MW00809509

by
Glynn MacNiven-Johnston

*All booklets are published thanks
to the generous support of the members
of the Catholic Truth Society*

ignatius press IHS CATHOLIC
TRUTH SOCIETY

CATHOLIC TRUTH SOCIETY
PUBLISHERS TO THE HOLY SEE

Table of Contents

All rights reserved. First published 2012 by The Incorporated Catholic Truth Society, 40-46 Harleyford Road London SE11 5AY Tel: 020 7640 0042 Fax: 020 7640 0046. Copyright © 2012 The Incorporated Catholic Truth Society.

ISBN 978 1 86082 808 9

Front cover image: *A Catholic Man kisses the coffin of Blessed Pier Giorgio Frassati at St Benedict's Church in Sydney* © DANIEL MUNOZ/Reuters/Corbis.

Introduction

In 2008, World Youth Day was held in Sydney, Australia, and hundreds of thousands of young people came from all over the world to participate. Among them was Pier Giorgio Frassati, an Italian from Turin. Unlike the others, though, he came in a one hundred and fifty kilogram zinc-lined coffin. He had died in 1925 at the age of twenty-four but the Australian Catholic Church held him in such high esteem as a patron of youth that they asked for him to be brought to Australia. The sealed casket remained in St Mary's Cathedral in Sydney for the time of the meetings (since World Youth Day actually lasts about a week) and many liturgies were built round his life and example.

This is the young man of whom Blessed John Paul II said, "Pier Giorgio was a young man overflowing with a joy that swept everything along with it, a joy that overcame so many difficulties in his life because the period of youth is also the time of trial and strength."

Family Background

To an outsider it might seem as if Pier Giorgio Frassati was born into a privileged life. His family was wealthy and successful with homes in Turin and Pollone. His parents were both high achievers. His father, Alfredo Frassati, a graduate in law, was a successful entrepreneur, the owner and editor-in-chief of a national newspaper. In 1895, aged thirty-six, he had bought a local paper called *Gazzetta Piemontese*, and transformed it into one of the first national newspapers in Italy, *La Stampa*. Pier Giorgio's mother, Adelaide Ametis, was a painter of some renown who had studied under Alberto Falchetti, a then-famous landscapist. She exhibited at national shows including several times at the Venice Biennale, and in 1912 one of her paintings was bought by King Victor Emmanuel III. But families are not always as they seem. Alfredo and Adelaide's marriage was extremely unhappy. They had married for love but soon discovered they had nothing in common, and their marriage became a battleground.

Childhood

The couple's first child, Elda, was born in 1899 but had died aged only eight months, and so it was with great joy that they welcomed their son and heir on 6th April 1901, which that year was Holy Saturday. Pier Giorgio was baptised immediately after birth as he was not breathing well. He was called Pier Giorgio Michelangelo. In fact, Alfredo had wanted the name Pietro after his father but Adelaide objected and they compromised by adding Giorgio. A year and a half later, Pier Giorgio's sister Luciana was born. These were the Frassatis' only children.

The two children were extremely close. They were thrown together as observers of their parents' volatile relationship. Luciana later described the atmosphere of their home as "an ill-defined nightmare". Meals were a special flashpoint, with Alfredo insisting that they eat dinner as soon as he returned from work, with no excuses and no delays. The tiniest infringement of his routine was met with enormous fuss. It was at this moment in the day that he would berate his wife for her inability to keep accounts, meaning that Adelaide would often run from the table in tears. Perhaps it was no wonder, then, that Adelaide preferred the company of her sister and emphasised more and more her identity as a member of the Ametis family. Alfredo dedicated himself to the newspaper, Adelaide dedicated herself to art; neither dedicated themselves to the children.

Strict parents

As parents, Alfredo and Adelaide were strict, even by the standards of the day. The children were kept at home in a rather claustrophobic atmosphere. They were never allowed out by themselves and when out with an adult they had to walk smartly and quickly, facing straight ahead and not looking round in a vulgar manner. Likewise, when at home, they were not to stand gawping out of the windows. Alfredo did play with the children when they were small, when he was at home, which wasn't often especially if the family were staying at the Villa Pollone, which, he was constantly being reminded, was the Ametis' family home and not his. It was this persecution of her father by her mother's family which drew Luciana to her father and he loved her in return. Since she was a girl he expected nothing of her and was therefore more able to accept her as she was. He found Pier Giorgio disappointing and slow and did not hold back from humiliating him in public. Pier Giorgio's future was set. He was heir to the newspaper. In fact, Luciana was everything Alfredo wanted in an heir, quick, clever and sophisticated, but there was never any thought that she could take over or even that she would ever work. Adelaide was closer to Pier Giorgio, but she was a mother who didn't allow any show of weakness in her son. She insisted that he excel, not waste time or daydream. More often than not, both Pier Giorgio and Luciana were treated as if they were nuisances. Luciana later described their daily life as "a sea of prohibitions". The children grew up starved of affection, starved of attention and sometimes even starved of food since their parents thought that was good for them. However, Luciana later wrote that their childhood taught them endurance and humility.

Schooldays and Faith

It is extraordinary, then, that Pier Giorgio loved life. He was a lively, active, noisy and fun-loving boy who attracted friends easily. He loved being outdoors and hated being cooped up inside. His mother encouraged him in his love of sport: climbing, skiing, riding, cycling - anything that was energetic. He was brave, too, and once saved a girl who was going to fall through the ice when they were skating.

The children were home-schooled at first, and when Pier Giorgio was eight, he asked their Latin teacher, a priest, to tell him the life of Jesus. The Frassati family was not very religious. Although recognised for his honesty, even-handedness and moral fibre, Alfredo was an agnostic. The Ametis family, meanwhile, would not have missed Mass but they were cynical about the faith and critical of the Church. Adelaide did not allow religion to interfere with life. She was a respectable Catholic but did not believe in exaggerating.

In 1908 both children failed their public exams. No one cared about Luciana's failure, but for Pier Giorgio, as the future director of *La Stampa*, to have failed, was considered catastrophic. Adelaide wrote to her sister that she did not know what would become of him. She feared for his future. He was seven.

The children were sent together to the local school, where Pier Giorgio gained a reputation for being a bit of a class clown, mainly because he was always the last to stop laughing and therefore the first to get caught. This only increased his parents' view that he was careless and feckless. Again in 1913 he failed, this time a Latin exam. Luciana passed, but no one cared. This latest exam failure was treated as if it were world-shattering, and Pier Giorgio wrote in a letter to his father, "I saw how upset Mama was and I thought about you being upset so much that I don't know how to say I'm sorry."

The children were then separated for the first time, and Pier Giorgio was sent to a strict Jesuit school, which, as far as his faith was concerned, was to turn out to be a blessing.

A maturing faith

It was at this Jesuit school that Pier Giorgio's faith was nurtured. He began to pray morning and evening. Once, his father found him asleep holding a rosary and, horrified that his son was being brainwashed, went to complain to the local priest. The priest, however, asked if Alfredo would prefer to find his son asleep over some trashy book, and Alfredo was silenced.

Adelaide was a very contradictory woman who taught her children to persevere in everything and never to give in to pain or tiredness but herself often over-reacted. She loved her son but was hypercritical of everything he did and understood him not at all. By the time Pier Giorgio was thirteen, Adelaide was terrified that he would become dissolute, even depraved, something which was very far from his character. She didn't want him to go to confession in case the confessor questioned him about impure thoughts and that somehow set him off on the path to becoming a sex-fiend. She was eventually reassured by the school chaplain. At the same time she opposed Pier Giorgio's request to be allowed to go to daily Mass and receive daily Communion, something he had been offered the opportunity to do at school but needed her permission for. She believed that going to daily Mass like a silly old woman would turn him into a narrow-minded fanatic. It took Pier Giorgio four days to get her to say yes. Perhaps it was as well she did not know that he alone of his class enjoyed the religious education lessons.

World War I

Despite being full of energy, Pier Giorgio found some of his life at this time very heavy. He was thirteen and felt overburdened by all he had to do. Some things he really hated. He especially loathed piano lessons, and on top of it all he had masses of schoolwork; but he persevered in all of it because this is how he had been brought up. Although he was in no way as stupid as his mother seemed to believe, he did not find school easy. His parents were disappointed in him for his lack of easy success and for getting into trouble for joking in class, but his teachers liked him on the whole and he was popular with the other boys. However, during World War I, political arguments began to erupt amongst the boys. Should Italy enter the war or not? *La Stampa* was against entering and so, therefore, was Pier Giorgio. The Assistant Editor of *La Stampa* also had a son, Camillo Banzatti, at the school and he too followed the same line as the paper. One day another boy (Mario Atilla Levi, who later became a distinguished historian) called Pier Giorgio and Camillo cowards and traitors like their fathers. Camillo immediately punched Mario and a fight started but Pier Giorgio didn't join in. When Pier Giorgio's parents heard about this they lauded Camillo as a hero but were mortified by Pier Giorgio's inaction and apparent lack of courage. If he could not even stand up for the family in this he was useless, he would never amount to anything. But Pier Giorgio was unmoved by the criticism, only saying that it would have been two against one and therefore unfair. As it was, Italy joined the war anyway.

Pier Giorgio felt the war very deeply and was once heard to say he would give his own life if it would stop the war. On a more practical note he began to help in the garden while the gardener was away at the front, and continued once he returned. Of course his parents didn't know anything about this. Pier Giorgio devised a way of waking early in the morning. He tied a rope to the leg of his bedside table and passed the rope out of the window. The gardener would pull on the rope and the shaking of the table woke Pier Giorgio up. Well, most of the time. Once the gardener had to pull the rope so hard the table fell over. The noise woke Adelaide but she, taking this as another example of Pier Giorgio's carelessness and thinking he had knocked the table over in the dark, told him next time to turn on the light.

Excessive prayer!

By this time Alfredo had become the youngest senator in Italy, which only served to emphasise what a disappointment Pier Giorgio was. And in 1918 he failed his exams again and had to stay on at school for another year. At this stage Pier Giorgio began to wonder if he had a vocation to the priesthood. This terrified his mother who already thought her son a fanatic. She was horrified at how often he said the rosary. She believed that saying the rosary once a year on All Saints' Day was more than enough. She was so upset by this behaviour that she had a priest come to visit Pier Giorgio. The priest told him it was unhealthy to pray so much. He should restrain himself and especially stop praying during the night. But Pier Giorgio was allowed to go to another Jesuit school. His mother was certain he would obey her and be less fervent. He spoke less and less at home and began spending a lot of time in his room. His parents believed he was studying; in fact, he continued to devote himself to prayer. He had so much, and so many people, to pray for.

Pier Giorgio had a deep personal prayer life but he also needed community of some kind. In 1922 he became a lay member of the Dominican Order. Their charism of preaching the gospel and combating heresy suited both his character and the times he was living in. He took the great religious and political reformer Savonarola as his patron. He also loved Thomas Aquinas, and St Catherine of Siena, whom he envied for her deep relationship with Christ.

His love of the Virgin Mary was evident in his devotion to the rosary, and he often visited a shrine in the mountains, the Sanctuary of the Black Madonna of Oropa. It is one of the oldest shrines to the Virgin in the Piedmont region. Like Pier Giorgio, she loves the mountains. A thousand years ago the monks tried to move her to a more accessible place but, it is said, after a short distance the three-foot-tall wooden statue became so heavy she couldn't be moved and they returned her to her chosen spot.

Love of neighbour

Pier Giorgio was always someone who noticed others. When he was a very young boy he went with his grandfather to visit a nursery school. It was lunch time and Pier Giorgio saw that one boy was alone. None of the others would sit near him or eat with him because he had a disfiguring skin disease. Quietly Pier Giorgio went to sit next to the boy and shared lunch with him. Another time Pier Giorgio noticed that the janitor at his school looked sad. He asked what had happened and discovered the man's son had died. Pier Giorgio comforted him, promised to pray for his son and remembered the anniversary of the boy's death too. He put others first. Even as a boy when he had a bad case of chicken-pox he chose to suffer from thirst all night rather than wake anyone and disturb their sleep. He had a desire to protect the weak. Luciana recalled that the only time he was ever really angry with her was when she abandoned one of their companions who was a poor skier so she could go off and enjoy skiing on the more difficult slopes.

Helping the poor

From a young age he wanted to help those less fortunate. Apparently, when he was only four years old, he opened the door to a woman begging. The woman was carrying her son, who was barefoot. Pier Giorgio's parents were out, but he gave the boy his socks and shoes since he had them to give and there was no one there to prevent it. At school he found an outlet for this desire to help the world. He joined the Society of St Vincent de Paul (SVP). From then on he was dedicated to helping the poor in any way he could. Pier Giorgio's days were filled with Mass, prayers, visiting and helping the poor and suffering, but this time he did manage to pass his exams. After finishing secondary school, Pier Giorgio entered the Royal Polytechnic Institute of Turin to study mining engineering. He had always had an interest in mineralogy but his real reason for choosing this subject was to "serve Christ among the miners". His family saw his choice of subject as irrelevant. His future was set. When he left university he would join *La Stampa*. In the meantime Luciana entered the Faculty of Law. Alfredo was happy she had followed in his footsteps, but nobody took her very seriously. Although *La Stampa* was a very liberal newspaper and her father published articles about the equality of women, no one expected Luciana to do anything other than marry well. She graduated with honours in 1923.

At university Pier Giorgio was derided for being a rich man's son, the son of a senator, but he gained the respect of his fellows for his calm and helpful manner. He joined various Catholic clubs and soon became one of the leaders. He also joined the pro-Catholic political party which was completely in opposition to the secular liberal party to which his father belonged. This was a big decision for Pier Giorgio, although Alfredo did not take it badly. Alfredo was much more concerned by what he saw as Pier Giorgio's fecklessness. He wrote to Pier Giorgio, "You must persuade yourself ... that life needs to be taken seriously. The way you behave will not do ... I have little hope you will change."

Secret charity

Meals remained a flashpoint in their home. Alfredo insisted on absolute punctuality and Pier Giorgio was often late. It never occurred to anyone to try and find out why, although if they had known they would only have taken it as further proof of his ridiculous way of behaving. In fact he was late because he had given away his tram pass and had to walk - or more usually run - home for meals. Pier Giorgio had no money of his own. Alfredo controlled every penny. Luciana was given a small allowance but nothing was given to Pier Giorgio. He was considered too hopeless. Alfredo had offered Pier Giorgio a choice of a car or some money when he graduated from secondary school. Pier Giorgio chose the money and quietly gave it away to the poor. His family believed he had just lost it, been tricked out of it or generally not looked after it properly. It is true that Pier Giorgio was sometimes exploited even by those who called themselves friends, but he never seemed to mind. On the contrary, he was looking after his money well by using it for the poor - even if it was morals that some of them were poor in.

Visiting the slums

Pier Giorgio believed deeply that Christ visited him every morning when he received Communion. He saw himself as emulating this when he visited the poor. He was very much at home in the slum districts. Friends who sometimes went with him were amazed: amazed that he was safe there, amazed that he chatted to these people as if they were his social equals. In fact, he admired them. He said, "Seeing that faith with which families daily bear the most atrocious sufferings for the love of God, makes me ask why I, who have so many things from God, have been so neglectful; why they who have not been privileged like me are so much better than me." When a companion asked him how he managed to ignore the filth around him he answered, "Don't forget that even though the house is sordid you are approaching Christ. Remember the Lord said, 'the good you do to the poor you do to me'. Around the poor, the sick, the suffering I see a light we don't have."

A friend wrote in his diary, "[Pier Giorgio] goes about in silence and secret without applause and gives both bread and his heart."

Practical help

Pier Giorgio was practical too and wanted people to be able to improve their lives themselves. For example, seeing a man begging he asked why he wasn't working. The man replied that he no longer had the tools of his trade, roasting and selling chestnuts. Pier Giorgio bought him the equipment he needed. He did this for many other workers too. He involved himself in people's lives. He was not just someone dispensing charity. He really wanted to help as a brother. For example, when he discovered an old woman who had been evicted, he not only found her another room but he, the son of a senator, carried her possessions through the streets, not caring who saw him. He became godfather to another woman's child. Her husband was often in prison for drunkenness so the next time the man was released Pier Giorgio met him at the prison gate and took him to find work at a factory where his criminal record would be overlooked.

The 'undeserving' poor

The poor often had to pawn things to keep going - even their clothes - and Pier Giorgio would redeem these things for them or pay the interest until they could redeem them themselves. He did not oversee their lives; he shared them. He was not even put off in 1918 when the Spanish Flu epidemic raged through Europe. He did not hesitate even to empty chamber pots and clean toilets. Some people in the SVP only wanted to work with those they saw as the deserving poor, but Pier Giorgio did not make distinctions. He was not scandalised by illegitimate children, broken families or criminality and thought his colleagues' distinctions were "not appropriate for today". But, of course he didn't judge his colleagues either, accepting that they were acting in good faith.

A friend remembered the day they visited the leper hospital together. They saw a boy of their own age and Pier Giorgio was deeply affected. He said, "Our youth and health should be put at the service of those who have neither." To do otherwise, he said, would be to despise God's great gifts. He was also very concerned to help demobilised servicemen but one of the places he most visited was the Cottolengo Hospital for the Mentally and Physically Handicapped. He stopped to talk to the patients (inmates would be a better description of their situation). He brought them sweets, clothes, money. He was really interested in them, really cared about them. He greeted them with a kiss as if they were his closest friends, never showing a hint of revulsion or worry he might catch something.

His faith was based on this love of neighbour. At a youth meeting he said, "Each of you knows the foundation of our faith is charity. Without it our religion would crumble. We will never be truly Catholic unless we conform our entire lives to the two commandments that are the essence of the Catholic faith: to love God with all our strength and to love our neighbour as ourselves ... With charity we sow the seeds of that true peace which only faith in Jesus Christ can give us."

Disdain for pomp and possessions

Pier Giorgio did not hold on to possessions. He owned very little but at one point he did own a bicycle. It took him a long time to save up enough money to buy it. He saved the small presents of money given by his relatives, and added to that the bits of money Luciana got playing a pickpocketing game with their father - not saying the money was for Pier Giorgio, of course. When he finally got the bicycle he was very happy and rode it everywhere. He often cycled the fifty miles between Turin and Pollone and at the end of the journey he would still have plenty of energy. One day the bicycle was stolen but Pier Giorgio was sanguine, saying someone else must have needed the bicycle more than he did.

At university he gave away his books to poorer students, saying he had too many. He gave away his shoes to someone who had none, and walked about in his slippers. He gave away any money he had. He even gave away his clothes.

A time in Germany

Pier Giorgio's father Alfredo was appointed Italian ambassador to Germany. Pier Giorgio, being at university, stayed in Italy living with his aunt, but he went to Germany for an extended visit. He arrived without a coat because he had given it away to someone he met on the train - he was travelling third class of course. He was worried that he wouldn't be able to keep up his care for the poor while he was in Berlin, but he met kindred spirits in Germany and continued visiting and helping the poor just as he had in Turin. The staff of the embassy were stunned to see Pier Giorgio take all the flowers from the embassy vases to put on the coffin of a beggar and collect up the left-overs from banquets to give to the poor. Luciana was a little frustrated with Pier Giorgio. He was a handsome young man who looked good in evening clothes and she wished he would join in more. Pier Giorgio just wasn't interested. Although he actually liked nice clothes he really hated getting dressed up and wasting time in that way. He wrote to his grandmother, "Thanks to the death of King Nicholas [the exiled King of Montenegro, who died in March 1921], they can't hold balls or big dinners which is just fine by me." Apart from anything else, he hated dancing. While he was in Germany he stayed for some time with the family of theologians Karl and Hugo Rahner, and it was there that he finally decided not to become a priest. Although priests were quite involved with the people in Germany, in Italy they were still isolated by too much deference. He felt that to help the poor he had to be able to be an ordinary person.

That is not to say Pier Giorgio spent all his time in Germany doing good works. He rode in the Tiergarten every day. He also toured round and visited galleries. Thanks to his mother he had developed a love and knowledge of art. He also went to the theatre and did touristy things. He was fascinated to meet some Japanese tourists whom he "bombarded with questions". And of course he visited churches and went to religious congresses. He had boundless energy and enjoyed life to the full.

Climbing and other sports

In case Pier Giorgio should seem impossibly holy, we should also note he loved sport, practical jokes and the company of friends. Pier Giorgio enjoyed the theatre but he always got the cheapest seats. If he was given better ones he would trade them in and give the difference to the poor. And, although this is often airbrushed from his photos these days, Pier Giorgio also smoked - sometimes a pipe and sometimes little Tuscan cigars - a habit he had picked up from his mother. He loved singing too and had a truly terrible voice. His friends would beg him to stop, but his exuberance could not be contained. He loved debating both religion and politics. He advocated radical change, supporting land reform; he wanted the land to go to those who worked it. He believed that students and workers should unite for a better future. Not everything was serious, though, and he and his friends were sometimes boisterous and loud enough to earn censure, but he was also cultured in the way his social class then was. He liked opera and could quote Dante.

Not all of Pier Giorgio's friends were such fervent Catholics but Pier Giorgio never hid his own practice. They all knew he went to Mass every morning and received Communion daily, saying it gave him the strength to fight inner battles against temptation and the strength to withstand adversity. He prayed openly in front of them and encouraged them to pray too. His friends and he would go climbing in the mountains and he would pray the rosary as they went. (He also offered to grease the boots of anyone who joined in.) "Learn to be stronger in spirit than in your muscles", he would say. "If you are, you will be real apostles of faith." Pier Giorgio loved the mountains, saying that the higher you went, the more clearly you could hear Christ's voice. Once the group reached the top they would have a ski race down. Even though one of his friends died climbing (not with Pier Giorgio), Pier Giorgio wrote, "I am keener than ever to climb mountains, reach the most difficult peaks, [because I] feel that pure joy is only to be had in the mountains". The last photo anyone took of Pier Giorgio is of him climbing. He wrote on the photo "Verso l'alto" - "towards the top" - and this phrase seemed to describe him and his life, not only towards the top of the mountain but towards heaven by a developed life of prayer. But even though he loved being in the mountains, Pier Giorgio often cut his holidays short in order to return to help the poor. If everyone was away, he said, who would look after those who were left behind?

Love and Sacrifice

One of the groups Pier Giorgio was in contained both men and women. This was very unusual at a time when clubs were normally either for men or for women. But Pier Giorgio was careful that all relationships remain platonic. That said he became very attracted to a maths student a few years older than himself. She was an orphan named Laura Hidalgo. He asked his mother to invite her and another friend to tea. His mother was happy to do this, as it did not occur to her in her wildest thoughts that Laura could be someone Pier Giorgio could love. Pier Giorgio himself gave no indication of his feelings to Laura either, as he was very careful not to cause her any pain. He wanted to be sure his family would accept her. His thoughts of course were of marriage. It became clear that his mother would never countenance his marriage with someone she considered so socially inferior and, not wanting to hurt anyone, he gave up this love. He was hurt though, and he couldn't even avoid Laura as she was part of his social circle. Quite why he gave up his own happiness is complicated. Partly he felt responsible for his mother. He saw she was her own worst enemy and he wanted to protect her. He also didn't want Laura to suffer rejection. He also believed that the life of a Christian was one of renunciation and sacrifice, but "this is not difficult if you think what these few years passed in suffering are, compared with eternal happiness where joy will have no measure or end and where we will have unimaginable peace".

Luciana was the only one he told of his feelings, but, he asked, how could he tear apart one family to create another?

Luciana's wedding

At this point he was really alone in his suffering. Luciana felt for him, but she had met a Polish diplomat called Jan Gawronski, and was busy with preparations for her wedding. Pier Giorgio wanted to find them a really special gift. After much searching, he finally bought them a beautiful antique ivory crucifix, which his family thought was a completely inappropriate present for a joyful occasion like a wedding. It was the custom to display all the presents with cards showing who they were from, and the family provided an official gift. An expensive silver tea service was displayed under Pier Giorgio's name and the crucifix remained in a box in the corner of the room. Luciana treasured the real gift though, and when the Gawronskis had to flee Warsaw in 1939, the crucifix was the only thing she took. After the wedding and reception, the family accompanied the newly-weds to the train station to set off on their honeymoon and from there to their new life outside Italy. Pier Giorgio shocked and embarrassed the family by bursting into tears. Although they were not so much together as they had been when they were children, Luciana and Pier Giorgio were deeply linked by their shared family experience. Pier Giorgio wrote to a friend, "I am happy because my sister is happy, the more so because her husband is good in the sense that you and I understand it. On the other hand the separation was terrible." Luciana too worried about Pier Giorgio, writing to him while she was on honeymoon to see how he was. He wrote in reply, "Any Catholic can't help but be happy ... Pain is not sadness which is a disease worse than any other ... so long as faith gives me strength I will always be joyful.".

Politics and Social Justice

In 1924, Pier Giorgio finally did something his mother approved of. Alfredo had resigned his ambassadorship. His politics were not popular with the Fascist government and a squad of thugs was sent to frighten the family by breaking into the house and causing damage. Pier Giorgio saw them off single-handedly, punching some of them and chasing them out of the house. Adelaide was proud. Pier Giorgio was embarrassed because accounts of the incident became public. He was not a coward and although he hated violence he was prepared to defend others. Pier Giorgio had become politically involved himself. He wanted to act against the system which neglected the poor. "Charity is not enough. We need social reform." he said. As well as being active in the pro-Catholic political party, he was involved in the Catholic Student Federation and Catholic Action.

Attacked by Communists and Fascists

He often accompanied priests who spoke in the communist areas of the city. This could end in their being attacked, but Pier Giorgio was not afraid. "When God is with us we need not be afraid." He did not instigate violence but he put himself in the way of it to defend others. Nor did he allow the threat of violence to stop him doing what he thought right. At this time, taking part in any kind of religious procession meant you risked being attacked by gangs of Fascists. Pier Giorgio and his father had in common their dislike of Fascism. He said, "At least [the communists] were for a great ideal, to raise the working classes who had been exploited for so long by people with no scruples. But what ideals do the Fascists have? ... They act induced only by money and dishonesty."

Catholic Youth

Large numbers of Catholic clubs and other organisations existed at that time and feelings ran high on all sides. They had their supporters too. Catholic train drivers arranged a special train on their day off to take groups from Turin to a Catholic Youth meeting in Novara. Pier Giorgio wanted to pay the drivers, but in order not to insult them he arranged a collection from all the passengers and then went up to the engine to place a bet he knew he would lose. He bet all the money he collected that the train could not go over sixty miles an hour and then lost the money to the drivers. Returning to the carriage he led his group in the Rosary. When they arrived at Novara they were attacked by a waiting Fascist group but they fought their way through.

Pier Giorgio was not a passive member of the organisations he belonged to, but a leader, and he often addressed the youth meetings. At one he said, "The times we are going through are difficult because cruel persecution of the church is raging. But you, bold and young people, should not be afraid of this small thing; remember that the church is a divine institution and cannot come to an end. She will last till the end of the world. Not even the gates of hell can prevail against her."

And at another, he said, "We, who by the grace of God are Catholics, must not squander the best years of our lives as so many unhappy young people do, who worry about enjoying the good things in life, things that do not in fact bring any good, but rather the fruit of immorality in today's world. We must prepare ourselves to be ready and handle the struggles we will have to endure to fulfill our goals. [...] But, in order for this to happen we need the following: constant prayer to obtain God's grace, without which our efforts are vain, organisation and discipline [...] and finally we need to sacrifice our own desires because without this we will not achieve our goal."

He was filled with zeal for the proclamation of the Gospel and the belief that as youth they could change the world.

With all these things, Pier Giorgio's life was full, and he kept putting off his exams. Finally, he only had two left, technology and "that disagreeable subject geometry". In the event, he never had to take them.

Death and Recognition

In June 1925, Adelaide's mother Linda became ill. She was ninety years old and was not expected to recover, so the family began to gather at the house in Turin. Things were already strained. Alfredo had decided he wanted a legal separation and Adelaide was terrified of the humiliation and public scandal. Pier Giorgio was feeling unwell with pains in his back, but all focus was on his grandmother. "Pier Giorgio could have chosen a better moment to be ill," his mother said. Pier Giorgio walked to church to call a priest for his grandmother before retiring to his room. The family went ahead with the Sacrament of the Sick without calling him, which upset Pier Giorgio very much. The family were just annoyed with him, not knowing he had dragged himself out of bed to sit with his dying grandmother. He was slowly becoming paralysed and was in terrible pain. Linda died and the funeral was at the family crypt in Pollone. Pier Giorgio was too ill to go. His mother accused him, "You are never there when you are needed." The family went to Pollone, except his mother who decided at the last moment to stay at home saying she was tired; and at last Pier Giorgio saw a doctor. He was critically ill with poliomyelitis which he had probably contracted in the slums. The virus enters the central nervous system and is fatal if it enters the brain.

Pier Giorgio spent five days in extreme pain, and doctors discouraged the family from coming near him. When his cousin did visit him, Pier Giorgio hid the seriousness of his situation so well that the cousin had no idea he was dying. Even Luciana had no idea and was anxious to return to her husband. Pier Giorgio was cared for by a nurse. In extreme pain he kept asking her "Will God forgive me?" Once they realised how seriously ill Pier Giorgio was, the family made every effort to save him. They would have sent to Paris for anti-polio serum but a storm made it impossible for the plane to take off. When it was clear he was dying, Pier Giorgio wanted to make his confession but his mother would have none of the priests he knew and worked with in the house. Instead she called one she approved of, and Pier Giorgio made his last confession to this priest, a man he had had a serious disagreement with.

Finally, Luciana was able to speak to her brother. He was concerned that people he was helping should not be abandoned. He gave Luciana someone's pawn ticket and a note to a friend with instructions about someone else's medicine. He told her where to find the notebook he wrote everything in. Luciana found Pier Giorgio had kept accounts detailed and careful enough to have satisfied even their father.

Pier Giorgio Frassati died on 4th July 1925. He was twenty-four.

When news of his death got out, people unknown to the family began arriving at the house to pay their respects. At first Adelaide tried to keep them out but Luciana persuaded her to let them come in, and when Pier Giorgio's body was taken from the house on the way to Pollone for the funeral, his parents were stunned to see the route lined by thousands of people, most of them from the poorest parts of Turin. People knelt along the street and others reached out to touch the coffin. Many of those he had helped had not even known the young man they saw walking through the slums praying the Rosary was the son of the Frassati family. Pier Giorgio was buried in the family crypt in Pollone. His mother decorated it with frescos.

In 1926, because he would not print pro-Fascist articles, Alfredo was forced to sell *La Stampa* for a nominal sum. He and Adelaide did not separate.

Luciana and her Polish husband, Jan, had six children. During World War II she obtained an Italian diplomatic passport and smuggled letters and documents into and out of Poland. She also managed to smuggle out people. Luciana died in 2007 aged a hundred and five.

The Cause of Pier Giorgio Frassati

Pier Giorgio's cause was opened in 1932. Things moved forward until 1941, when an anonymous source cast doubt on his morality. The issue was that he went climbing in the mountains in mixed company. The cause was put on hold but still his fame spread. In Poland, the young Karol Wojtyła was among those inspired by him. Visiting Pier Giorgio's tomb in 1989, and now Pope John Paul II, he said, "In my youth I felt the beneficial influence of his example and as a student I was impressed by the force of his Christian testimony." Many years later Luciana began to negotiate to clear her brother's name. Her purpose was not to have the cause re-opened but to restore his reputation. The allegations were refuted and the beatification cause was re-opened in 1978. A miracle which had taken place in 1933 was officially accepted. This was the cure of forty-year-old Domenico Sellan from tuberculosis of the spine. He was paralysed and near death when a priest brought him a small prayer card of Pier Giorgio Frassati. Domenico was miraculously cured and lived another thirty-five years. In 1981 Pier Giorgio's body was found to be incorrupt. One witness said, "His body was perfectly preserved. He had a smile on his face and a rosary in his hands. It was like meeting him for the first time."

Pier Giorgio was beatified in 1990. Pope John Paul called him the "Man of the Eight Beatitudes". His body was transferred to Turin Cathedral and his feast day is 4th July.

At the time of the beatification, the then Master of the Dominicans said of Pier Giorgio, "His understanding of himself as a person called to holiness in virtue of his baptism and confirmation gives witness to the very theology of the laity that we find in the Second Vatican Council. His ministry and spirituality were centred on the Eucharist and helping the poor. His prayer life was of an austere nature which was in a way driven by his great love of Jesus and Mary. But this love was not limited to a false piety which finds comfort only in oneself. His prayer was a call to action ...

"If like Blessed Frassati you embrace the ministry of the laity ... the world will surely be a better place in the twenty-first century".

Prayers

Prayer for the Canonisation of Pier Giorgio Frassati

O merciful God,
who through the perils of the world
deigned to preserve by your grace
your servant Pier Giorgio Frassati
pure of heart and ardent of charity,
listen, we ask you, to our prayers and,
if it is in your designs that he be glorified by the Church,
show us your will,
granting us the graces we ask of you,
through his intercession,
by the merits of Jesus Christ, Our Lord, Amen.

IMPRIMATUR, 1932: ✠ Maurillo, Archbishop of Turin

Litany of Blessed Pier Giorgio Frassati

(For private devotion)

Lord, have mercy. *Lord, have mercy.*
Christ, have mercy. *Christ, have mercy.*
Lord, have mercy. *Lord, have mercy.*

God our Father in heaven, *have mercy on us.*
God the Son, Redeemer of the world, *have mercy on us.*
God the Holy Spirit, *have mercy on us.*

Holy Trinity, One God, *have mercy on us.*
Holy Mary, *pray for us.*
All the angels and saints, *pray for us.*

Blessed Pier Giorgio, *pray for us.*
   (Repeat after each invocation.)
Loving son and brother,
Support of family life,
Friend of the friendless,
Most Christian of companions,
Leader of youth,
Helper of those in need,
Teacher of charity,
Patron of the poor,
Comfort of the sick,
Athlete for God's kingdom,
Conqueror of life's mountains,
Defender of truth and virtue,
Opponent of every injustice,
Patriotic citizen of the nation,
Loyal son of the Church,
Devoted child of the Madonna,
Ardent adorer of the Eucharist,
Fervent student of the Scriptures,
Dedicated follower of St Dominic,
Apostle of prayer and fasting,
Guide to a deep love for Jesus,
Diligent in work and study,
Joyful in all of life's circumstances,

Strong in safeguarding chastity,
Silent in pain and suffering,
Faithful to the promises of Baptism,
Model of humility,
Example of detachment,
Mirror of obedience,
Man of the Beatitudes,

Lamb of God, you take away the sins of the world,
have mercy on us.
Lamb of God, you take away the sins of the world,
have mercy on us.
Lamb of God, you take away the sins of the world,
have mercy on us.
Pray for us, Blessed Pier Giorgio Frassati,
That we may be made worthy of the promises of Christ.

Let us pray:
Father, you gave to the young Pier Giorgio Frassati the joy of meeting Christ and of living his faith in service of the poor and the sick. Through his intercession, may we, too, walk the path of the Beatitudes and follow the example of his generosity, spreading the spirit of the Gospel in society. We ask this through Christ our Lord.
Amen.

IMPRIMATUR, November 2, 1994:
✠ Joseph A. Galante, D.D., J.C.D., Bishop of Beaumont, TX

Pope John Paul II's Homily
from the Beatification Mass
of Blessed Pier Giorgio Frassati

"I will ask the Father, and he will send you another Advocate to be with you always, the Spirit of truth" (*Jn* 14:16). During the Easter season, as we progressively draw near to Pentecost, these words become more and more timely. They were spoken by Jesus in the Upper Room the day before his Passion, as he took leave of his Apostles. His departure - the departure of the Beloved Master through his death and resurrection - prepares the way for another Advocate (*Jn* 16:7). The Paraclete will come; he will come precisely because of Christ's redemptive departure which makes possible and inaugurates God's new merciful presence among people. The Spirit of Truth, whom the world neither sees nor knows, however, makes itself known by the Apostles, because "it remains with them and will be in them" (cf. *Jn* 14:17). And everyone will become witnesses to this on the day of Pentecost.

Pentecost, however, is only the beginning, because the Spirit of Truth comes to remain with the Church for ever (cf. *Jn* 14:16), endlessly renewing itself in future generations. Therefore the words of the Apostle Peter are addressed not only to the people of his day, but also to all of us and our contemporaries. "Sanctify Christ as Lord in your hearts. Always be ready to give an explanation to anyone who asks you for a reason for your hope" (*1 P* 3:15). In our century, Pier Giorgio Frassati incarnated these words of St. Peter in his own life. The power of the Spirit of Truth, united to Christ, made him a modern witness to the hope which springs from the Gospel and to the grace of salvation which works in human hearts. Thus he became a living witness and courageous defender of this hope in the name of Christian youth of the twentieth century.

Faith and charity, the true driving forces of his existence, made him active and diligent in the milieu in which he lived, in his family and school, in the university and society; they transformed him into a joyful, enthusiastic apostle of Christ, a passionate follower of his message and charity. The secret of his apostolic zeal and holiness is to be sought in the ascetical and spiritual journey which he travelled; in prayer, in persevering adoration, even at night, of the Blessed Sacrament, in his thirst for the Word of God, which he sought in Biblical texts; in the peaceful acceptance of life's difficulties, in family life as well; in chastity lived as a cheerful, uncompromising discipline; in his daily love of silence and life's "ordinariness". It is precisely in these factors that we are given to understand the deep well-spring of his spiritual vitality. Indeed, it is through the Eucharist that Christ communicates his Spirit;

it is through listening to the word that the readiness to welcome others grows, and it is also through prayerful abandonment to God's will that life's great decisions mature. Only by adoring God who is present in his or her own heart can the baptised Christian respond to the person who "asks you for a reason for your hope" (*1 P* 3:15). And the young Frassati knew it, felt it, lived it. In his life, faith was fused with charity: firm in faith and active in charity, because without works, faith is dead (cf. *Jm* 2:20).

Certainly, at a superficial glance, Frassati's lifestyle, that of a modern young man who was full of life, does not present anything out of the ordinary. This, however, is the originality of his virtue, which invites us to reflect upon it and impels us to imitate it. In him faith and daily events are harmoniously fused, so that adherence to the Gospel is translated into loving care for the poor and the needy in a continual crescendo until the very last days of the sickness which led to his death. His love for beauty and art, his passion for sports and mountains, his attention to society's problems did not inhibit his constant relationship with the Absolute. Entirely immersed in the mystery of God and totally dedicated to the constant service of his neighbour: thus we can sum up his earthly life!

He fulfilled his vocation as a lay Christian in many associative and political involvements in a society in ferment, a society which was indifferent and sometimes even hostile to the Church. In this spirit, Pier Giorgio succeeded in giving new impulse to various Catholic movements, which he enthusiastically joined, but especially to Catholic Action, as well as Federation of Italian Catholic University Students, in which he found the true gymnasium of his Christian training and the right fields of his apostolate. In Catholic Action he joyfully and proudly lived his Christian vocation and strove to love Jesus and to see him in the brothers and sisters whom he met on his way or whom he actively sought in their places of suffering, marginalisation and isolation, in order to help them feel the warmth of his human solidarity and the supernatural comfort of faith in Christ.

He died young, at the end of a short life, but one which was extraordinarily filled with spiritual fruits, setting out for his "true homeland and singing God's praises."

Today's celebration invites all of us to receive the message which Pier Giorgio Frassati is sending to the men and women of our day, but especially to you young people, who want to make a concrete contribution to the spiritual renewal of our world, which sometimes seems to be falling apart and wasting away because of a lack of ideals. By his example he proclaims that a life lived in Christ's Spirit, the Spirit of the Beatitudes, is "blessed", and that only the person who becomes a "man or woman of the Beatitudes" can succeed in communicating love and peace to others. He repeats that it is really worth giving up everything to serve the Lord. He testifies that holiness is possible for everyone, and that only the revolution of charity can enkindle the hope of a better future in the hearts of people.

Yes, "tremendous are the deeds of the Lord. Shout joyfully to God all you on earth" (*Ps* 66:1-3). The verse of the Psalm resounds in this Sunday liturgy as a living echo of young Frassati's soul. Indeed, we all know how much he loved the world God created! "Come and see the works of God" (*Ps* 65/66:5): this is also an invitation which we receive from his young soul and which is particularly addressed to young people. Come and see God's "tremendous deeds among men" (ibid.). Tremendous deeds among men and women! Human eyes - young, sensitive eyes - must be able to admire God's work in the external, visible world. The eyes of the spirit must be able to turn from this external, visible world to the inner, invisible one: thus they can reveal to others the realm of the spirit in which the light of the Word that enlightens every person is reflected (cf. *Jn* 1:9). In this light the Spirit of Truth acts.

This is the "inner" person. This is how Pier Giorgio appears to us. Indeed, his entire life seems to sum up Christ's words which we find in John's Gospel: "Whoever loves me will keep my word, and my Father will love him, and we will come and make our dwelling with him" (*Jn* 14:23). This is the "inner" person loved by the Father, loved because he or she has loved much! Is love not possibly what is most needed in our twentieth century, at its beginning, as well as at its end? Is it perhaps not true that the only thing that lasts, without ever losing its validity, is the fact that a person "has loved"?

He left this world rather young, but he made a mark upon our entire century, and not only on our century. He left this world, but in the Easter power of his Baptism, he can say to everyone, especially to the young generations of today and tomorrow: "You will see me, because I live and you will live" (*Jn* 14:19).

These words were spoken by Jesus Christ when he took leave of his Apostles before undergoing his Passion. I like to think of them as forming on the lips of our new Blessed himself as a persuasive invitation to live from Christ and in Christ. This invitation is still valid, it is valid today as well, especially for today's young people, valid for everyone. It is a valid invitation which Pier Giorgio Frassati has left for us.

Further Reading and Information

Further Reading

Frassati, Luciana, *A Man of the Beatitudes* (San Francisco, Ignatius Press, 2001)

Frassati, Pier Giorgio, *Letters to his Friends and Family* (New York, Alba House, 2009)

Lorenzo, Maria di, *Blessed Pier Giorgio Frassati* (Boston, MA, Pauline, 2004)

Organisations

The St Vincent de Paul Society (SVP)

The St Vincent de Paul Society was set up in the nineteenth century by Blessed Frederic Ozanam, taking inspiration from the life and work of St Vincent de Paul. Its main aims are showing love to your neighbour through personal contact, and alleviating poverty. A large part of its work is visiting the sick, lonely, housebound, imprisoned. www.svp.org.uk

Pier Giorgio Frassati Societies

Since the establishment of the Associazione Pier Giorgio Frassati in Italy in 1990 various societies promoting the spirituality of Pier Giorgio Frassati among young people have sprung up round the world. Piergiorgiofrassati.org

Frassatiusa.org

For UK societies contact info@frassati.co.uk

Lay Dominicans

www.laydominicansuk.com

www.3op.org

REAL LOVE

Mary Beth Bonacci

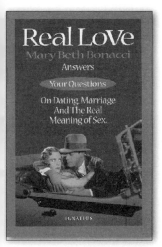

From the hundreds of real questions she gets at teen conferences, popular youth speaker and columnist Bonacci provides 225 questions and her in-depth answers based on Church teaching on dating, marriage and sexuality. Through these questions and her answers, Mary Beth offers a comprehensive catechesis of the Church's teaching in the areas of marriage and human sexuality.

RL-P . . . 322 pp, Sewn Softcover, $14.95

Maria Goretti

Teenage Martyr

In 1902 in an Italian village a young girl, Maria Goretti, was murdered during a sexual attack. Her killer, Alessandro Serenelli, himself a teenager, was a close neighbour well known to her and her family. He had been threatening her for some time. What does it mean, how can it help, to say that she is a virgin and martyr? This is an often misunderstood and sentimentalised story. When many parents and teenagers strive for a balanced view of sexuality, of personal integrity, of Christian family life, and forgiveness to those who do irreparable harm, Maria's story speaks powerfully and authentically. It echoes John Paul's cry to today's youth – 'Do not be afraid to be saints!'

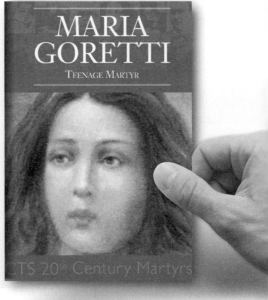

CTS:B398-P ISBN 978 1 86082 025 0 www.ignatius-cts.com

The Song of Bernadette

The classic film that beautifully portrays the appearance and miracle of Our Lady of Lourdes, and the life of the girl to whom Our Lady appeared, St. Bernadette. This film won five Academy Awards, including Best Actress for Jones as Bernadette, and Best Score.

📀 SONG-M . . . 156 min., $19.95

Bernadette
150th Anniversary Edition

From Jean Delannoy, one of France's foremost filmmakers, comes this top quality feature film production of the story of St. Bernadette and the apparitions of Our Lady of Lourdes."Shot on location in France with outstanding cinematography and a beautiful music score, this is the film that was chosen to be shown daily at the shrine in Lourdes.

📀 BER2-M . . . 120 min., $19.95

The Song of Bernadette
Franz Werfel

The classic literary depiction of the life of Bernadette, written by Werfel to fulfill a promise he made to God while fleeing the Nazi persecution of Jews.

SONG-P . . . 605 pages, Softcover, $19.95

🕮 **ignatius press**
www.ignatius.com • 1-800-651-1531

A Way of Life for Young Catholics

An Introduction to the Catholic Faith

Written for young Catholics who want to live their faith more deeply but are not sure what steps to take, this booklet contains practical, down-to-earth advice on many aspects of daily life, whether spiritual (prayer and confession) or moral (alcohol and drugs, dating and chastity) or emotional (coping with worry or suffering) or vocational (discovering my vocation, finding a good husband or wife). It will be especially helpful for older confirmation candidates, students, and young adults hoping to learn more about their faith.

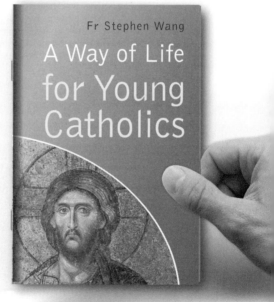

CTS:DO774-P   ISBN 978 1 86082 487 6   www.ignatius-cts.com

YOUCAT

Christoph Cardinal Schoenborn

YOUCAT is short for Youth Catechism of the Catholic Church, which was launched on World Youth Day, 2011. Developed with the help of young Catholics and written for high-school age people and young adults, YOUCAT is an accessible, contemporary expression of the Catholic Faith. The appealing graphic format includes Questions-and-Answers, highly-readable commentary, summary definitions of key terms, Bible citations and inspiring and thought-provoking quotes from Saints and others in the margins. What's more, YOUCAT is keyed to the Catechism of the Catholic Church, so people can go deeper.

Introducing the __FREE__

LIGHTHOUSE CATHOLIC MEDIA
— BIBLE APP —

- **Complete text of the Old and New Testament (RSV-CE)**
- **Dramatized audio New Testament—FREE audio of the entire Gospel of John**
- **10 hours of FREE audio commentary from Dr. Scott Hahn**
- **Over 50 Lighthouse talks available for purchase**

 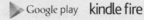

Search "Lighthouse Bible" in the App Store

THE LOSER LETTERS

Mary Eberstadt

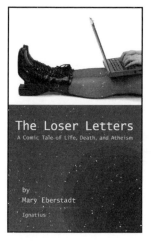

Amid the many current books arguing for or against religion, social critic and writer Mary Eberstadt's *The Loser Letters* is truly unique: a black comedy about theism and atheism that is simultaneously a rollicking defense of Christianity.

Echoing C.S. Lewis' *Screwtape Letters* and Dante's *Divine Comedy*, Eberstadt takes aim at bestsellers like *The God Delusion* and *God Is Not Great* with the sexual libertinism their authors advocate. In her loveable and articulate tragic-comic heroine, A.F. Christian, Dawkins, Hitchens and the other "Brights" have met their match.